Pebble Books are published by Capstone Press
151 Good Counsel Drive, P.O. Box 669, Mankato, Minnesota 56002
http://www.capstonepress.com

1 2 3 4 5 6 09 08 07 06 05 04

Library of Congress Cataloging-in-Publication Data
Townsend, Emily Rose.
    Deer / by Emily Rose Townsend.
        p. cm.—(Woodland animals)
    Includes bibliographical references and index.
    Contents: Deer—Where deer live—What deer do.
    ISBN 0-7368-2067-1 (hardcover)
    1. Deer—Juvenile literature. [1. Deer.] I. Title.
QL737.U55T69 2004
599.65—dc21   2003010738

Note to Parents and Teachers

The Woodland Animals series supports national science standards
related to life science. This book describes and illustrates deer that
live in woodlands. The photographs support early readers in
understanding the text. The repetition of words and phrases helps
early readers learn new words. This book also introduces early
readers to subject-specific vocabulary words, which are defined in
the Glossary. Early readers may need assistance to read some words
and to use the Table of Contents, Glossary, Read More, Internet
Sites, and Index/Word List sections of the book.

Woodland Animals

Deer

white-tailed deer

by Emily Rose Townsend

Consulting Editor: Gail Saunders-Smith, Ph.D.
Consultant: William John Ripple, Professor
Department of Forest Resources
Oregon State University

Capstone
press

Mankato, Minnesota

Table of Contents

Deer

Deer are mammals
with hoofed feet.

mule deer

Deer have long legs
that help them move fast.

mule deer

Most male deer grow antlers on their heads.

white-tailed deer

Male deer shed their antlers every year. They grow new antlers each spring.

white-tailed deer

areas where deer live

Where Deer Live

Deer live in many areas around the world. Many deer live in woodlands.

What Deer Do

Deer often look for food at dawn or dusk.

black-tailed deer

Deer eat leaves, flowers, grass, twigs, and bark.

white-tailed deer

Deer often stand still when they sense danger.

white-tailed deer

20

Deer run fast
to escape danger.

white-tailed deer

Glossary

antlers—bones that grow on the top of a male deer's head

dawn—the time when light first appears in the morning

dusk—the time when the sun begins to set in the evening; many deer look for food at dawn and dusk because they blend in to the surroundings; other animals cannot easily see deer at dawn and dusk.

hoofed—having a hard covering over an animal's foot; deer have two hooves on each foot.

mammal—a warm-blooded animal with hair or fur; a female mammal feeds milk to its young.

shed—to have something fall or drop off; deer shed their antlers every year.

woodland—land covered mostly by trees; woodlands are also called forests.

Read More

Berendes, Mary. *Deer.* Naturebooks. Chanhassen, Minn.: Child's World, 2000.

Johnson, Jinny. *Deer.* Busy Baby Animals. Milwaukee: Gareth Stevens, 2001.

Murray, Julie. *Deer.* Animal Kingdom. Edina, Minn.: Abdo, 2003.

Internet Sites

FactHound offers a safe, fun way to find Internet sites related to this book. All of the sites on FactHound have been researched by our staff.

Here's how:

1. Visit *www.facthound.com*
2. Type in this special code **0736820671** for age-appropriate sites. Or enter a search word related to this book for a more general search.
3. Click on the **Fetch It** button.

FactHound will fetch the best sites for you!

Index/Word List

Word Count: 80
Early-Intervention Level: 13

Editorial Credits

Mari C. Schuh, editor; Patrick D. Dentinger, designer; Scott Thoms, photo researcher;
  Karen Risch, product planning editor

Photo Credits

Corbis, 12, 20
Corel, 6, 16
Dwight R. Kuhn, 10
Eda Rogers, 4
Housterstock/Dave G. Houser, 14
Lynn M. Stone, 18
Red Clover Studio/Jill Castiglia, 1
Thomas Kitchin/Tom Stack & Associates, 8
Tom & Pat Leeson, cover